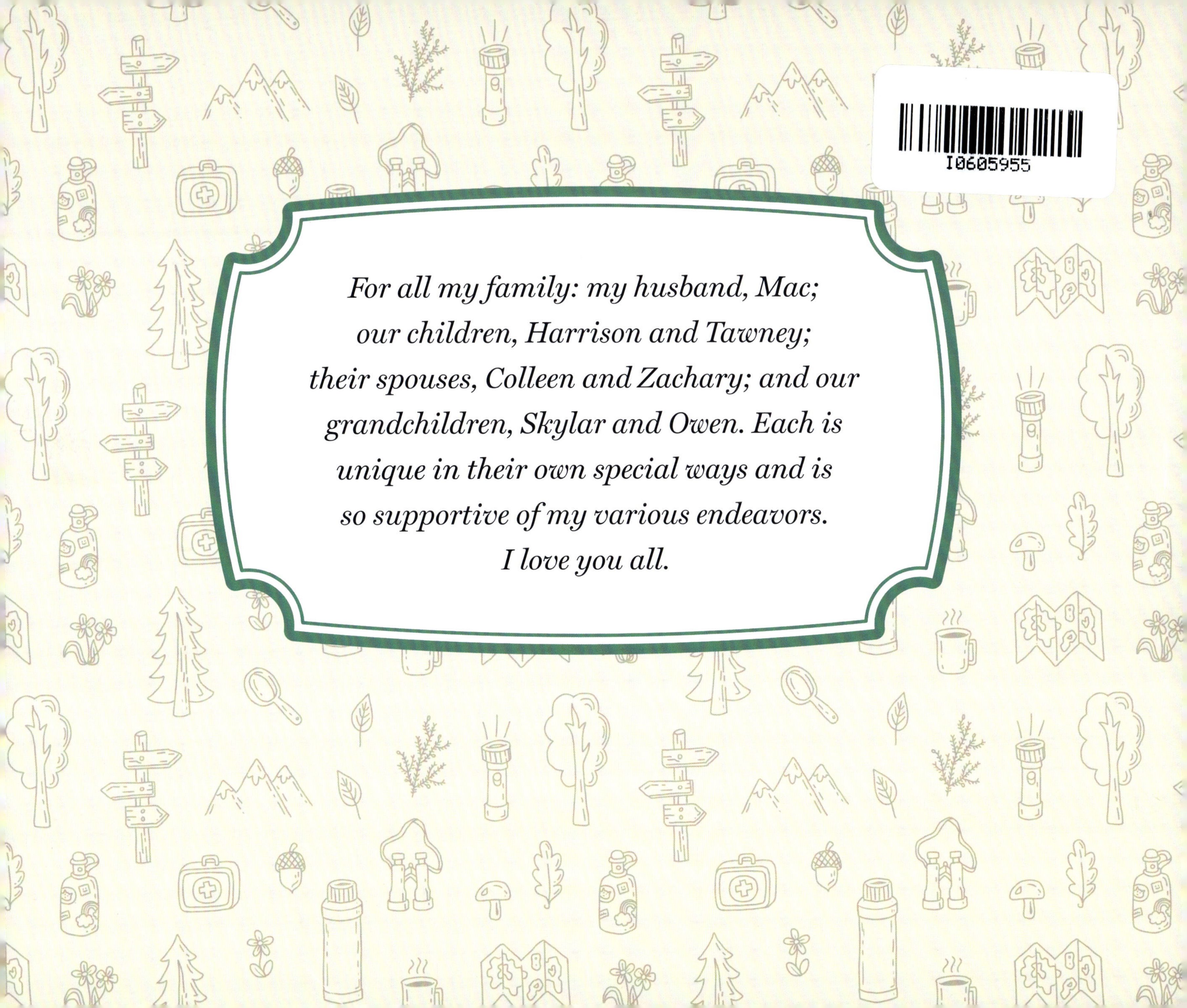

For all my family: my husband, Mac;
our children, Harrison and Tawney;
their spouses, Colleen and Zachary; and our
grandchildren, Skylar and Owen. Each is
unique in their own special ways and is
so supportive of my various endeavors.
I love you all.

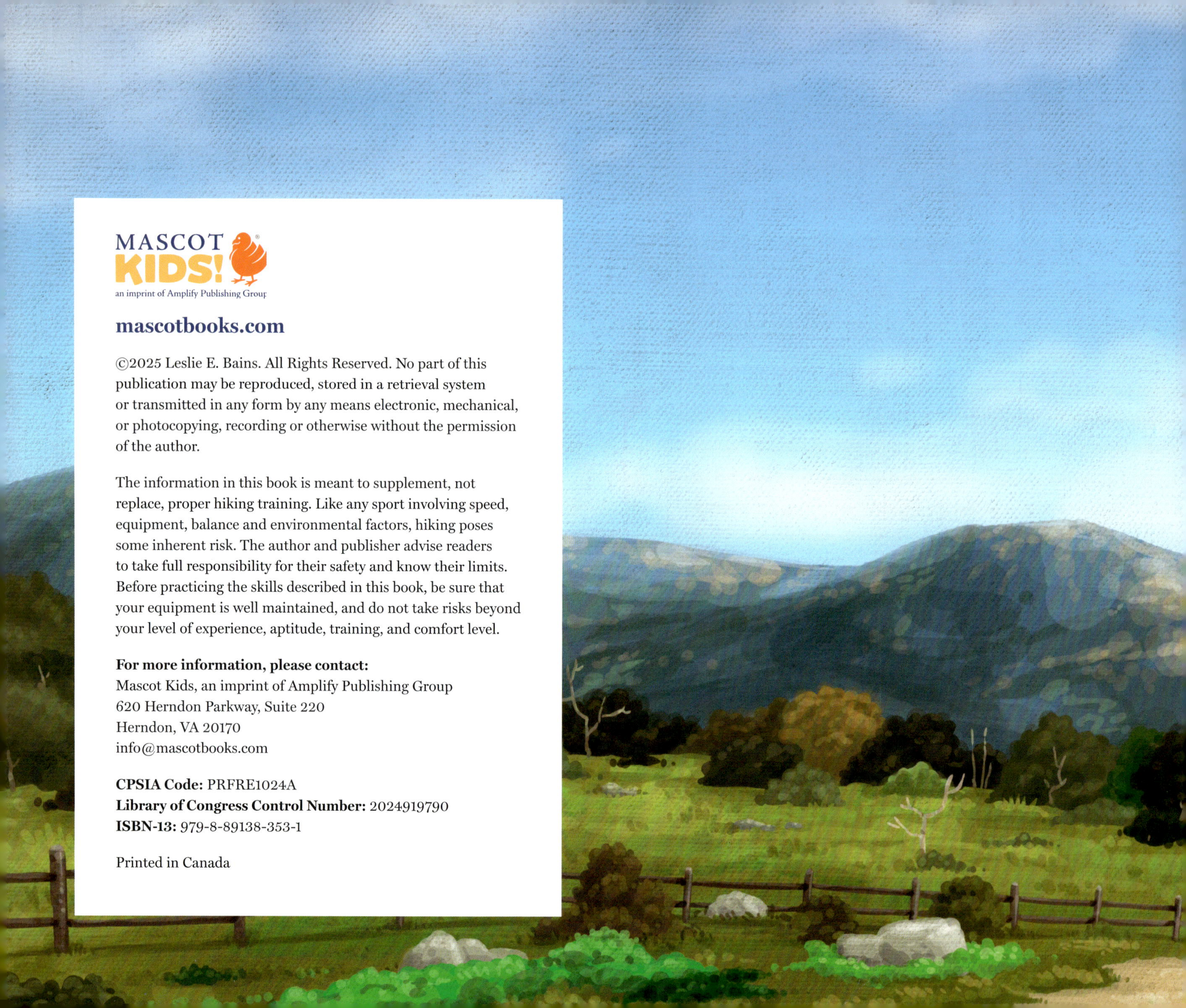

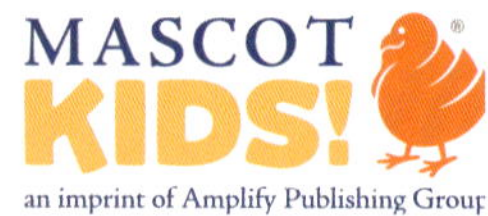

MASCOT KIDS!
an imprint of Amplify Publishing Group

mascotbooks.com

The information in this book is meant to supplement, not replace, proper hiking training. Like any sport involving speed, equipment, balance and environmental factors, hiking poses some inherent risk. The author and publisher advise readers to take full responsibility for their safety and know their limits. Before practicing the skills described in this book, be sure that your equipment is well maintained, and do not take risks beyond your level of experience, aptitude, training, and comfort level.

For more information, please contact:
Mascot Kids, an imprint of Amplify Publishing Group
620 Herndon Parkway, Suite 220
Herndon, VA 20170
info@mascotbooks.com

CPSIA Code: PRFRE1024A
Library of Congress Control Number: 2024919790
ISBN-13: 979-8-89138-353-1

Printed in Canada

BIRDS, MONARCH BUTTERFLIES, and SHORT HIKES in the Santa Barbara Area

Leslie Bains

Illustrated by Danny Moore

TABLE OF CONTENTS

INTRODUCTION

When I glance out a window or take a hike, stunningly simple memories come to mind. I observe a hummingbird flapping its wings seventy times per second or four thousand wingbeats per minute, a monarch butterfly swooping onto a eucalyptus tree leaf to renew its life cycle, or simply walking on a trail in the woods or on a beach. All of these brief moments leave me with a smile. For me, every day brings a special moment.

I divided this book into three sections: a family guide to the various types of seasonal birds in the Santa Barbara community; an overview of the tens of thousands of monarch butterflies who inhabit our area from November to late February; and a variety of short hikes in the hills, on the beach, or in a number of environmental habitats, which include some unique museums in this area.

There is a Latin phrase that says: *Solvitur Ambulando*. It means "solved by walking." At the end of this book, I have included questions you can ask your children to engage their minds as well as their feet. Please enjoy exploring the many moments in this book!

NOTES
30
15

ESSENTIALS TO TAKE WHILE EXPLORING

Water, water, and more water

Hat

Sun protection if you are outdoors

Decent shoes—a pair of sneakers is fine

Bug spray if you are outdoors

Small daypack

Leash for your dog when hiking and bags to pick up after them

Small pad to take notes, if you wish

A BRIEF HISTORY OF SANTA BARBARA

Santa Barbara is located about ninety miles north of Los Angeles. The city lies between the soaring Santa Ynez Mountains and the Pacific Ocean. The climate is described as Mediterranean with many sunny days. Santa Barbara is often referred to as the American Riviera with warmer winters and cooler summers.

In addition to being a popular tourist destination, Santa Barbara has a vibrant economy that includes schools and universities, healthcare, agriculture, and technology.

The Chumash Indians were the earliest known residents of the area, followed by various explorers and then Spanish missionaries, who arrived in 1782. The missionaries built twenty-one missions in California from San Diego to Sonoma. The Santa Barbara Mission is the only one with twin bell towers, and it also has a Moorish fountain and an original aqueduct that is still used by the City of Santa Barbara.

Just before the beginning of the twentieth century, Californians discovered oil. By 1903, they had become the largest oil-producing state. The country's first offshore oil development was made off the coast of California, and some of the oil rigs can still be seen off Santa Barbara's coast. Many of the oil rigs are nearing the end of their useful lives. Today, California only produces about 3 percent of the oil in the United States.

In the 1950s and 1960s, the population of Santa Barbara surged. Between the four thousand foot mountains and the Pacific Ocean, the topography of the land—scrub brush (chaparral), oak trees, and sandy soil—creates an ideal backdrop for Santa Barbara. It inhibits dramatic growth, maintaining the beauty of the city without urban sprawl. The number of residents in Santa Barbara is about eighty-five thousand to ninety thousand.

THE ESSENTIALS OF BIRDWATCHING

What to do:

- Pick a spot and stand still for a few moments. More birds can be seen this way.
- Look at the bird's size, shape, and color. Many birds have different colors on their heads, breasts, wings, and tail feathers.
- Don't get too close, as the bird may fly away. Listen to sounds the bird makes. Each bird makes different sounds. Some make a loud noise to protect their nests; some call out to their friends to say, "I am here! Where are you?"
- If the bird is flying in the sky, follow it with your eyes. It might be looking for its nest or something to eat.
- The habitat or environment of a bird can tell you a great deal about it. Sometimes birds only spend the summer or warmer months in a certain area. Then they fly south, migrating to find a place for food and warmer air during the winter.

THE BEACH AND SHORE BIRDS

Habitat: The beach is a border between the ocean and land with sand or rocky areas. The waves pound the beach, breaking up the rocks and seashells into little pebbles and tiny grains of sand. Grasses grow in between sand dunes to protect the birds and their nests. There are many types of animals and insects that live on the beach, including crabs, insects, beetles, worms, and sand clams. Birds circle above and land on the sand, looking for a meal or to make a nest.

Beach birds, like gulls, are mainly found on the coast, and they need a good food supply. They eat almost anything, including fish, shore bird eggs, small reptiles, spiders, dead things that wash up on shore, crabs, and snails. Gulls generally build their nests on the ground and lay their eggs out in the open or at the base of a small beach shrub.

The **Herring Gull** or **Western Gull** are two of the most familiar gulls. They have webbed feet, pink legs, and a yellow bill with a tiny, red dot. They are usually found in larger groups along the shoreline.

Heermann's Gull are not seen in the winter. They have a white head, gray back, and black feet.

Other shore birds have longer legs than gulls and are fun to watch. They run in and out of the ocean as the waves ebb and flow. They stab small crabs, sea urchins, snails, and worms with their strong bills. The American Oystercatcher is easy to spot because it has a long, bright-red bill, yellow eyes, all-black body, and pinkish legs. It can open clams and oysters with its long bill.

Black Oystercatcher—Their yellow eyes are very bright.

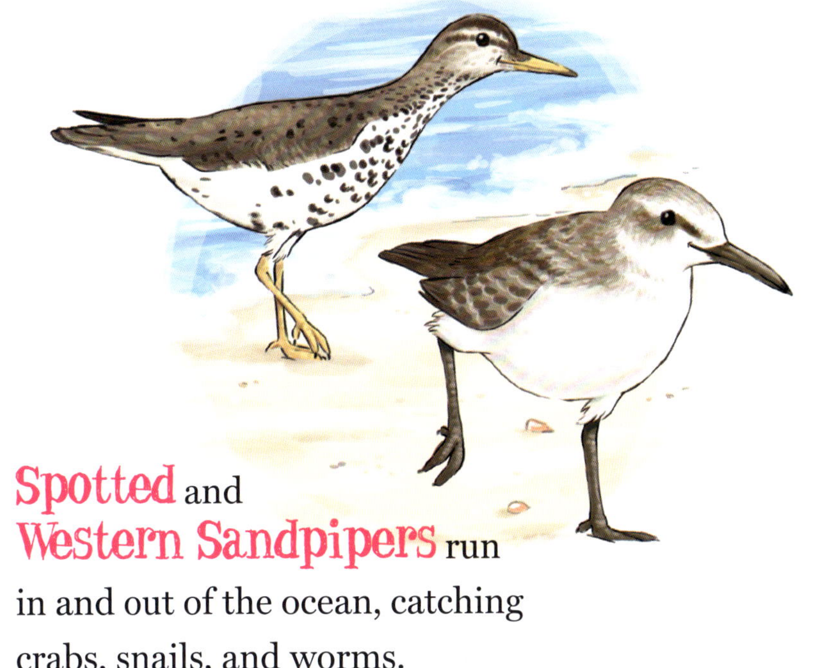

Spotted and **Western Sandpipers** run in and out of the ocean, catching crabs, snails, and worms.

THE BACKYARD BIRDS

Outside your window, you can find many birds. If you have room, I recommend getting some bird feeders: one with tiny holes for small birds; one with regular-sized holes; and most importantly, a hummingbird feeder. You can buy an inexpensive one online and fill the container with sugar water. Because of its climate, Santa Barbara has lots of hummingbirds, which especially can be seen in the spring and fall. They feed on a variety of flowers, and because of their fierce wing activity, sometimes they need to feed every ten or fifteen minutes. Here are a few of the types you will see:

The Hummingbirds

The **Ruby-Throated Hummingbird** is very small and beats its wings three hundred times a minute. They go flower to flower and also feed at feeders filled with sugar water.

Anna's Hummingbird has a red crown and a red-spotted throat with dark-green feathers.

Allen's Hummingbird has a green back and rusty-colored sides.

The Black-Chinned Hummingbird has a black throat, white chest, and greenish feathers.

THE YEAR-ROUND RESIDENTS

The **Crow** and the **Raven** look somewhat alike and will take over a feeder, chasing the small birds away. They eat anything and make loud noises: "Caw, caw." You might see or hear these two birds any day.

The **Red-Tailed Hawk** is about twenty to twenty-five inches long. You can often see it circling in the sky looking for something to eat. It eats rabbits, squirrels, rodents, bird eggs, and lizards. It has a dark brown back, a white neck and front, and a wide red tail.

The **Scrub Blue Jay** can be seen year-round. Its head, wings, and tail are blue, and its throat and breast are white.

The **Acorn Woodpecker** has a bright red head, white throat and forehead, and black wings and tail. You will see the woodpecker on the sides of trees looking for insects. If you are quiet, you can hear its rat-tat-tat!

THE SPARROWS

You will always see sparrows. The most common are the House, Chipping, and Song Sparrows. Sometimes they are hard to tell apart.

THE OWLS

Great Horned Owl

Western Screech Owl

Barn Owl

These are the three most common owls to see. You can find them right before dark or just before the sun comes up. They can see in the dark, but a little moonlight helps. Move your flashlight up and down the branches of a tree. You will be able to see them when the light catches their eyes.

OTHER POPULAR BIRDS BY SEASON

Spring

The **Black-Headed Grosbeak** is about seven inches long with a black head and rusty orange collar and breast. You will see it in large trees and thick bushes.

Summer

The **Hooded Oriole** is bright yellowy-orange and black. They hang upside down to get nectar from flowers.

Fall

The **Western Tanager** is very colorful with a bright red head, yellow body, and black feathers. They are generally found in fir trees eating fruits and insects.

Winter

The **Dark-Eyed Junco** is about five to six inches long. Its eyes, head, and throat are black, and it has a white breast and grayish tail.

A STORY ABOUT HARRY THE HAWK

Why doesn't anyone like me? Why doesn't anyone like me?

I am a hawk, a raptor. I am about twenty inches tall with large wings and a long tail. I have excellent eyesight to help me find food. Like the raptor dinosaur, I eat meat like lizards, mice, snakes, little chicks, and eggs from birds' nests. Maybe that is why no one likes me.

Whenever I fly around way up in the sky, flapping my large wings and looking for food, the other birds start screeching. "There is Harry the Hawk—watch out! Sit on your nest to protect your eggs or little chicks."

I glide through the air and then swoop down very fast to grab my food with my feet, which are called talons. Birds are always screeching at me.

I want other birds to like me, but I have to gather food to feed my family. Why don't they understand me?

One beautiful, sunny summer day, I was flying near a big beach. There were so many people on the wide sandy beach having picnics and building sandcastles. Some were playing volleyball and frisbee, and others were tossing big, colorful beach balls. Teenagers were surfing on the waves, and children with their parents were running in and out of the water, jumping up and down along the shoreline, yelling for joy when they were knocked over by a wave.

I watched one family with three children having such a good time. They were sitting under their big beach umbrella drying themselves off after being in the ocean. Then, I saw their two-year-old boy in blue swimming trunks and a bright yellow hat pick up his little shovel and pail and start walking away from his family. No one noticed him as he walked close to the water's edge. He wanted to play in the waves again and build a sandcastle. *Oh my*, I thought. *No one is watching this cute little boy as he is getting closer and closer to the ocean.*

He stuck his toes in the water as the waves went back and forth. I thought, *He is going to be knocked over and carried out to sea by a big wave.* What could I do?

I dove down toward the little boy, flapping my wings very hard and screeching with my voice: "Caw, caw, caw!" It is a terrifying sound. I kept cawing, and finally, people on the beach looked up in the sky. They saw me diving down at a great speed toward the little boy. The parents looked up and saw their boy was in danger. They ran down to the shoreline and grabbed the boy just as a bigger wave was about to knock him over. Then, I looked up and heard people saying, "The hawk saved the little boy. Did you see how the hawk saved him?" I made a circle in the sky and dove down one more time to the cheers of the beachgoers. I was a hero.

The next day in the newspaper, the headline story was about a hawk who saved a little boy at the beach from being hurt. As I swooped around at the end of the day looking for food, other birds chirped and nodded their heads, thanking me for saving the little boy. Maybe this was a new day for hawks. We can be very helpful too.

THE MONARCH BUTTERFLY

Every fall and winter, tens of thousands of monarch butterflies migrate southward from Canada and the Rocky Mountains to escape the cold weather and winter storms. Twenty thousand to twenty-five thousand butterflies come to Goleta Butterfly Grove, which is also known as the Ellwood Main Monarch Aggregation, from early November to late February. It contains the largest concentration of monarchs in California. The name "monarch" is believed to have been given in honor of King William III of England, whose reign lasted from the late 1600s until 1702. He was also known as the Prince of Orange.

You can reach the Goleta Butterfly Grove two ways. First, the Sperling parking area at 7729 Hollister Avenue is about a half-mile walk to the Butterfly Grove. Second, some people park in the neighborhood on Coronado Street and walk a short distance on a marked path to the Grove. The eucalyptus trees have suffered recently from California's extended drought and from beetles, but the City of Goleta is working to enhance the habitat, preserve the area, and improve its trails.

The following pages show the life cycle of the butterfly, in which they undergo a complete metamorphosis. Their transformation takes anywhere from twenty-five days to seven weeks, depending on the extremes of the weather. The four stages are the egg, the larva (caterpillar), the pupa (chrysalis), and finally the adult butterfly.

Egg
Caterpillar
Butterfly
Chrysalis

THE LIFE CYCLE OF THE MONARCH BUTTERFLY

Mating: The male monarch approaches the female by touching her head with his wing, and then the female flutters to the ground. The male monarch has two black dots on its orange wings.

Egg: The female lays an egg on the underside of a milkweed or eucalyptus leaf.

Larva (Caterpillar): In two to five days, the larva emerges and eats the egg for its first meal. The caterpillar grows one to one and a half inches over the next two weeks.

Chrysalis: The caterpillar forms a small hanging sac called a chrysalis or pupa, and the butterfly starts to form and grow inside. In about eight to twelve days, the butterfly emerges.

Butterfly: Some butterflies live for fifteen to twenty-nine days, while others live for up to six months.

Another place to see a variety of butterflies, in addition to monarchs, is the Santa Barbara Museum of Natural History. Every summer, the curator brings over one thousand butterflies from Costa Rica. The museum builds a huge, tented garden, and the butterflies flutter freely for several months. There are over two dozen species to see. The exhibit is open from Memorial Day to Labor Day.

SOME SHORT HIKES

Outlined below are a few short hikes to be enjoyed on different terrains.

Distance:
3 miles; 4.83km

Butterfly Beach

This beach is located in Montecito near the Music Academy of the West. Many residents bring their dogs (on a leash) for the three mile walk along the pristine shoreline. Besides swimming, sunbathing, and surfing, beachgoers enjoy trying to spot dolphins and whales in the distance. The Channel Islands can be seen from here, as they are just twenty miles out to sea. The beach has an east-west orientation, which allows for some spectacular sunrises and sunsets. There are no restaurants or food vendors, so pack a sandwich and enjoy a picnic.

Santa Barbara Botanic Garden

The Santa Barbara Botanic Garden is seventy-five acres and contains over one thousand species of plants. There are almost six miles of hiking trails over various landscapes. After paying your admission fee, pick up a free map of the various trails. There are also free guided tours at various times. Dogs on a leash are welcome, and do bring a picnic lunch.

I recommend turning right over the small bridge at the entrance and walking up the left-hand side of the meadow toward the redwood grove. This path will take you to the Mission Dam, built in 1806. Do stop and take the loop through the Redwood mini-forest. The redwoods were planted over one hundred years ago, and the tallest one is close to 163 feet tall. Redwoods capture more carbon dioxide than any other tree and are less susceptible to climate change. They thrive in our foggy climate, and some grow to over 250 feet high.

Now you will want to walk to the well-marked Mission Dam. Under the direction of the Franciscan Fathers, the Chumash people built the dam to furnish water to their village, the fields, and the Mission, which is about two miles below. The aqueduct is a perfect example of gravity at work and is part of Santa Barbara's water system today.

There are over eleven sections of the Botanic Garden, including the Japanese Teahouse and the desert area, and offers an opportunity to hike in the backcountry.

The Museum of Natural History

Let's go back thousands of years and see some dinosaurs. At the Museum of Natural History there is a short, fun walk along Mission Creek with replicas of five giant dinosaurs and four smaller ones. As you approach each dinosaur, it will roar and bring you back in time. The fourth floor of the museum has an extensive collection of dinosaur skeleton specimens.

Santa Inez Mountains

Lastly, let's take a hike up to the hills of the Santa Inez Mountains.

This twenty-five-acre park is located in the San Roque Canyon off of Canon Drive. There is lots of parking further down the road on the right. The park offers many adventures, as the park serves as the trailhead for several local, longer hiking trails. The area was a farm until the late 1920s, when it was sold and then scheduled to be a golf course and country club until the Great Depression in the 1930s. The land was donated to Santa Barbara and named in honor of Ralph Stevens. He was a landscape architect who contributed his skills to many projects in the city.

As you enter, there are shaded picnic areas, a large playground, barbecue grills, and restrooms. The 1.6-mile round-trip hike is perfect for people of all ages. It ends at the Lauro Canyon Reservoir. You will see flowering meadows, sycamore and oak trees, and the San Roque Creek that flows through the park. Children love to wander down to the creek and toss loose stones in the stream. There is a wooden bridge on your left that leads to a grassy field. Dogs are welcome but must be on a leash.

QUESTIONS FOR CHILDREN

Questions

1. *Can you name two types of shore birds?*
2. *What bird has a red tail and saved the little boy?*
3. *What bird goes rat-tat-tat?*
4. *What kind of bird would you see at dusk?*
5. *What color is a monarch butterfly?*
6. *Who was the monarch butterfly named after?*
7. *What are the four stages of the monarch butterfly's life cycle?*
8. *What is the tallest tree in the Botanic Garden?*
9. *What year was the Mission Dam built?*
10. *How many dinosaurs are by Mission Creek?*

Answers

1. *Either a Herring Gull, Western Gull, Heermann's Gull, Sandpiper, or an Oystercatcher*
2. *A Red-Tailed Hawk*
3. *An Acorn Woodpecker*
4. *An owl*
5. *Orange*
6. *King William III of England*
7. *Egg, caterpillar, chrysalis, butterfly*
8. *The redwood tree*
9. *1806*
10. *There are nine dinosaurs on Mission Creek*

ACKNOWLEDGMENTS

When I arrived in Montecito, my new friend and next-door neighbor, Ilene Nagel, said "Let's take a hike." When I saw her poles, hiking boots, and outfit, I said to myself, "This is a professional hiker." I gracefully passed on her offer, but her spirit encouraged me to write a West Coast children's hiking book to complement my award-winning Nantucket hiking book. I would also like to thank Dr. Alice Kanevsky and her young son, who pointed the way to several hikes appropriate for children.

Once again, my husband marched on some hikes with me and viewed the butterflies. Our son, Harrison, and his wife, Chaz, explored the Goleta Butterfly Grove, watching thousands of monarch butterflies begin their life cycle. Our daughter, Tawney, has continued to provide editing advice and encouragement.

Mascot Kids and their illustrator, Danny Moore, are the glue that keeps the project moving along.

Thank you all!

ABOUT THE AUTHOR

Leslie E. Bains is a resident of Montecito, California. An award-winning children's book author, Leslie had a distinguished fifty-year career in private banking and investments. She was the highest-ranking woman as senior executive vice president of HSBC. Leslie was also president of AFS International, the largest student exchange program in the world with offices in over fifty countries.

Throughout her career, Leslie has been involved as a corporate director and trustee of many companies and nonprofits. She is currently on the boards of The Granada Theatre and the Santa Barbara Cancer Foundation. She is also on the board of Duke University Global Health and Duke University Health System.